Inside The Chi-Lites Music

Darren Cubie

Revised Special Edition

Copyright © 2023 All Rights Reserved.

In Loving Memory of my father, Creadel Jones

Print ISBN: 979-8-218-26044-6

Contents

Dedication 5
Overview of the Chi-Lites Music 7
The Rehearsal 9
FBI & IRS Corruption 13
Family Drama 19
Money Is The Root Of All Evil 25
Gang Activity & Intimidation 31
Royalty Theft 37
The Business Proposal/ Celebrity Run-Ins 41
A Cry for Help 47
Entertainers Against Exploitation & Corruption 51
Paternity Court TV 55
Run-In With Justin: Part 1 59
Jail Time 63
Run-In With Justin: Part 2 66
Acknowledgments 71
About the Author: Darren Cubie 72

Dedication

I dedicate this book to the legendary exploited entertainers and our families who struggle to stop legacy abuse throughout entertainment and music. I would also like to dedicate this book to my father, Creadel Jones, from the Chi-Lites, and his wife and widow, Deborah Jones, my mother.

To all those who believe in justice, equality, honesty, integrity, and great entertainment: with unity and reform, we can work together for a brighter tomorrow and a rewarding future.

Overview of the Chi-Lites Music

The way we look and the talents we have are God-given. However, *how* we use those talents is what defines our journey. Being a born star does not guarantee an easy route. To make a mark in a world where hundreds of thousands of talented individuals strive to shine, indeed it takes determination and hard work to be amongst the few who are to be remembered for centuries.

My father, Creadel "Red" Jones, was amongst the few who managed to cast a solid impression on the music industry. Even though he lived a life different from what he deserved, his contribution to the music world will never be forgotten.

It all started in 1959, in his final year of high school. He along with my mother, Deborah Jones, and friends Robert Lester and Marshall Thompson performed in a band that went by the name of the Chi-Lites. Together, the band members attended Hyde Park High School in Chicago, Illinois. The band produced numerous songs that locked spots in the Top 10 Hits, Top Singles, and the Billboard Hot Chart 100.

The group with Robert Lester and Eugene Records was originally named Chanteurs, which was renamed shortly after my father and Marshall Thompson joined. Originally, Marshall and my father were in the group Desideros. Its new name was the Hi-Lites.

Unfortunately, the name had to be changed again because it turned out that the Hi-Lites was already registered to someone else. The band members found a way of recognizing their hometown and changed it to the Chi-Lites. Marshall was responsible for managing the group, fellow group member Eugene Records wrote several songs, and my father was the bass-baritone singer. Although Eugene wrote the majority of the songs, there were several others that the group wrote together.

Undisputedly, the Chi-Lites ruled the R&B industry for decades.

"Let Me Be The Man My Daddy Was" was the first song that served to be the band's claim to fame. The group had a long list of singles that were sung and enjoyed by fans of R&B music. The first song that made it to the top hit charts was "Give More Power to the People." "Oh Girl" was their second single selling over three million copies, and the list just goes on and on.

In 1968, the Chi-Lites signed a contract with Brunswick Records and the songs they produced under this label took them to new heights of popularity. About eight years later, in 1978, my father began having some issues being part of the band. In no particular order, this book will outline the different issues and problems faced not only by my father but by the Chi-Lites music group, my family, and myself as well.

The Rehearsal

One day, the Jackson 5 came to our house for a "rehearsal." That's what they called it. They were asked to go into the house to pick my dad up and practice a while before the world tour with the Chi-Lites. All five members—Randy, Jermaine, Jackie, Marlon, and Tito—were there. They arrived together in a black limousine while Michael arrived in a separate one. They parked in front of our house, walked in, and began to talk about how they were going to produce this concert and what they needed to make it a memorable one.

I believe that Tito, Joe Jackson, and Jermaine Jackson asked my father for $50,000 because they needed the money to spot the instruments. They were either leasing the instruments or needed to buy new ones for the concert. So, my dad gave Joe $25,000 upfront and told him he would give him the rest later. The next day, I remember seeing the Jacksons going downstairs to do a rehearsal for the concert. They even had dinner at our house.

During the session, my sisters and I---when were nine, six, and I was five--were brought down to the entertainment room located in the bottom basement of our house. My mother was down there at first, but she ended up going upstairs. All four members of the Chi-Lites—including my dad, Marshall Thompson, Eugene Record, and Robert Lester—were there, along with the owner of Brunswick Records, Nathan "Nat" Tranopol. Also, there was Joe Jackson, each of the Jackson 5, including Randy, Jermaine, Jackie, Marlon, and Tito, and Michael.

None of the others caught our attention as much as the new figure, whom none of us recognized, who came with Nat. It was a priest dressed in a satanic black robe with a hood that covered his face. The downstairs area was one large entertainment room with two smaller rooms that are connected to it. The main room had a pool table and bar while the other two rooms were simply sitting rooms. There was also a small half-bathroom to the side.

As I walked into one of the sitting rooms, I saw my sister being bent over the table and raped by Marshall Thompson from behind while Joe Jackson pinned her down. Once he finished, Marshall got up and then began to hold my sister down by her shoulders while Joe Jackson then began to savagely rape her from the front. The other Jackson 5 members and the Chi-Lites musicians were in the loop in the entertainment room, waiting right next to this room we were in.

I tried to stop them, but I was held down by the Jackson 5 members. I started to yell, "Get off my sister! Get off my sister!" but they weren't bothered one bit. I was quickly subdued by the group who then brought my sister into the main entertainment room where a satanic pentagram was drawn on the floor in white chalk.

They took off all my sister's clothes and placed her on the table at the altar they had created. Then, the Jackson 5 members, one by one, began to rape my sister. Each of the Chi-Lites members, including my father, raped her next. To make matters worse, as they were holding me down, they raped me as well. All 12 of them were animals, as they raped me one by one. It was truly a terrifying experience.

I was able to escape and go upstairs. From the top of the stairwell, I could see the black-hooded priest walking behind Joe and Marshall as they were escorting my sister out of the room where they had just raped her. The satanic priest had a Caucasian infant in his arms, who looked to be only about two months old.

Joe Jackson reached under the altar and came back up with a dagger and a gold goblet adorned with jewels and rubies. In one swift motion, Joe put the baby on the altar and held it down, while Marshall slit the baby's neck. Then, Joe Jackson placed the goblet underneath the child's neck and collected its blood.

I watched in horror as the baby died soon after having its throat slit. Joe took the blood-filled cup, drank some of it, then passed it around to the other people in the room. He first passed it to the members of Jackson 5, who were each in black robes. Each member took a sip and passed it to the next person. Nat Turnopol and the satanic priest took a sip as well. Soon, it was the members of the Chi-Lites' turns to drink from the cup.

They were all dressed in red robes, and each member took a sip, including my father. I couldn't bear to watch anymore.

When I closed the basement door, my mother told me to go upstairs to my room. As I made my way through the kitchen, I saw my mother opening the refrigerator. It was the type that had a freezer on one side and the refrigeration on the other. The freezer area of the fridge was stuffed with at least six dead babies, excluding the baby I had just seen them murder. The babies were wrapped in plastic, and it was a horrific sight. There were even small bodies wrapped in plastic on the counter. I asked my mother what it was, just to confirm I wasn't losing my mind. She blatantly said, "Dead babies." I began crying, unable to believe what I had just heard, but her expressions were blank, stern, and emotionless. She asked me to go to my room upstairs as if I was crying over something petty and not something inhumane.

Over the next few days, I witnessed Joe Jackson and Marshall Thompson cut the bodies of the babies they had slaughtered to please their satanic god. They cut their legs and arms off, placed the limbs in a baking dish, then began to eat the cooked babies' remains. It took me days to overcome the trauma. The shock and horror from everything I witnessed solidified the pain I felt from what was happening.

FBI & IRS Corruption

Soon after the incident, my father left with members of his band and the Jackson 5. As soon as he returned from the tour, he was greeted by the FBI. Basically, the FBI contacted my dad and my mother to inform them that the record company he was associated with was under investigation for tax evasion, audits of frogman money laundering, racketeering, illegal wiretapping, and drive reports. The FBI wanted to know more about what the affiliation was with the New Jersey mafia while seeking insights into the organized crimes that were happening.

Joe Jackson, Nat Tarnopol, and Marshall Thompson were the ones who told my dad not to give any information in reference to the connection to the Chicago Mafia or the Decavalantees, which was a New Jersey organized crime family ran by Simone Decavalantees other names. The FBI wanted to know about Sunny (Getaon Vastola), Nat Tarnopol, Marshall Thompson, Carl Davis, Murray Hill, Melvin Moore, Peter Cards, Vice President Lee Shep, Irvin Wigan, and Nancy and Donna.

So, Nat and Marshall came by the house and had a long discussion with my mother and father, telling them not to answer any questions. Additionally, they suggested that my father open up a trust fund account following the concert performance. They had tours and concert events worldwide that they were to perform throughout Europe and other parts of the world. Some concerts were also to be held in various cities in the United States.

If I recall correctly, the Chi-Lites performed with the Jackson 5 and Michael Jackson in 1983 for the Triumph Tour. They earned $30 million from their world tour concert performances, including their performance with the Jackson 5. My father received $5 million from that and put his share into a trust fund account as he was told. Of that $5 million, he put $3.5 million into multiple child trust fund accounts with Bank of America so the IRS could not obtain the money out of it. My portion of the money was $300,000. My sister's portions were $250,000 each.

Because of tactics like these, the IRS and the FBI were investigating the executive of Brunswick Records and Nat Tarnopol because they felt that the company was involved in bribery and pirating.

They considered the entire thing to be fraud, assuming or rather knowing that the royalties of artists were compromised and that the record money was part of a money laundering scheme. This was how the IRS's criminal investigation was caught in the case.

The situation escalated when Jackie Wilson came onto the scene. It was said that he owed the IRS a great deal of money, and the only way he could have a settlement was by testifying against Brunswick Records and their owner Nat Tarnopol. This was around the same time that my father was approached for investigation. The FBI and IRS wanted my father to testify against them too, which resulted in our family life getting extremely affected in all the wrong ways. It wasn't an easy decision to agree to testify against criminals. Of course, it was going to have its consequences, which is why Dad was very skeptical about it.

The people he sought unwanted counsel from weren't any of his well-wishers. We had people coming into our house every day, discussing with Dad what statement he should have recorded with the FBI. This wasn't the extremity of this situation, but it was the beginning of the havoc that followed.

My father didn't want to become weak by avoiding the right thing to do, but he had a family to provide for. His decision was going to affect us all. When Marshall and Tarnopol sensed that their convincing wasn't reaping anything positive, the mob got directly involved. The debates changed into threats, and there came a point when members of the mob were inside our house, pointing a gun at me and my sister. They told Dad that if he testified against them, we'd die.

Given how the situation was slipping out of hand, my mother urged my father to testify. She believed it was best to seek protection from the law instead of surrendering to the mafia goons. The federal agent on the case assured Dad that he would be able to protect our family through the witness protection program, but the way things were unfolding, it was difficult to pick sides.

When the mafia discovered that my dad was thinking of making a deal with the federal agents, they began threatening us in any way that they could. Once, they put a dead horse in my parents' bed to scare us. In all honesty, Mom had freaked out. I mean... why wouldn't she? Dad contacted the police and the FBI, and they immediately came. Then, they'd often throw dead fish on our driveway to scare us. They even went as far as planting a bomb under our house.

Each time, Dad contacted the law for help. I remember how a SWAT team had arrived along with a bomb defusal squad. We were asked to stay in the house until we were told it was all clear. After an hour or so, we were given a green signal to exit the premises of our house, which was after the team had managed to defuse the bomb successfully.

It was traumatizing to see how we were attacked. As children, my sisters and I had no idea what was happening. We were just scared to the core and wanted it all to end. However, wanting was not enough alone.

* * *

Throughout the IRS and FBI investigations, the criminal activities of Marshall Thompson and Nat Tarnopol were never discovered. This is because of corrupt investigation agents working with both agencies, who failed to find any evidence. The federal agents, jury, and even the judge had been found guilty of taking bribes of over $10.5 million.

The leading agent from both agencies took the evidence and destroyed it. It contained important information about drug trafficking mafias consisting of hundreds of millions of dollars in cocaine and heroin being trafficked at the hands of both Marshall Thompson and Nat Tarnopol. What was included in the evidence was their involvement in drug smuggling operations with organized mafia crime members of both the New Jersey crime family, the Chicago crime family of Illinois, and their frequent smuggling of hundreds of millions of dollars that would go through their hands to Brunswick Records.

I remember witnessing cocaine kilos which were stacked from floor to the ceiling, with rooms and closets stuffed with noticeable items, including refrigerators. Millions of dollars from kilos of cocaine were being trafficked by Marshall Thompson to the Decavalcantee organized crime family and the Chicago organized crime syndicate.

The drug traffickers would send it to the New York crime mafia families throughout New York and eventually distribute it to their clients. The FBI had been monitoring our homes and every movement we made but still allowed hundreds of millions of dollars worth of cocaine trafficked and frequent trips by leaders of organized crime families throughout New Jersey, Chicago, and New York to occur.

They frequently visited our home and Marshall Thompson's home for drug trafficking. Marshall Thompson was responsible for most of the drug smuggling done by the Chi-Lites, along with Brunswick Records. I think one of the biggest questions to me was how leading FBI investigators were monitoring our house, Marshall Thompson's house, and Brunswick Records, but were allowing leaders of organized crime families to come and go at will, with hundreds of millions of dollars of cocaine visually able to be seen smuggled inside and outside of the homes of Marshall Thompson and Nat Tarnopol.

Despite being under constant FBI surveillance, which included foam tabs, bugging, camera surveillance, and FBI patrol vehicle tails, which followed us everywhere, we went, not to mention the helicopter surveillance, there was no justice. Despite my efforts to stop royalty theft and report Brunswick Records, the FBI would deliberately refuse to effectively investigate the corruption of Brunswick Records or Marshall Thompson.

In fact, I was even told by the Detroit FBI office not to call or report any activity involving royalty theft of Bank of America, child trust fund theft involving Marshall Thompson, or the relatives of my father's trusteeship theft and attempted account theft involving the hiding of over $875,000 of my own trust fund money. They also told me not to call about the additional $3.5

million in trust fund money related to the children of Creadel Jones, which was rightfully ours but was stolen by Marshall Thompson.

***

So, the FBI investigators and federal judges, along with IRS criminal investigations agents, wasted no time attempting to blackmail The Chi-Lites, Marshall Thompson, and Brunswick Records. IRS officials came by our house to obtain a bribe from each of the Chi-Lites members, including my father, and the Brunswick Records executives for $2.5 million. On the second visit, the FBI claimed to have some audio recordings of my father containing sensitive information. They said they even knew how much money the group members had earned through the concert. The FBI threatened my father that if he did not testify against the criminals, they would make sure he, along with the other members of the band involved, would be put behind bars. My father didn't respond much. He just listened to what they said and watched them leave the house.

Shortly after the FBI left, we had more visitors. This time around, it was the IRS. The IRS took a step further and pointed guns at my sisters and me saying that dad needed to either give them the $2.5 million they had, or they were going to kill us. After taking our lives, they said they'd prosecute him, the Chi-Lites musician, and the Brunswick Records executives. They were straight away asking for bribery, both the FBI and the IRS.

My mother and father had a meeting with Marshall Thompson and all the others, which included members of the Chi-Lites and executives of the record company. They went to the court building to see the judge in his office. It was where my father and Marshall delivered the $2.5 million and then some in a briefcase to the judge. I'm not exactly sure how much it was, but it included money for the jury as well.

So, the judge was bribed with another $3.5 million along with the FBI, which also was $3.5 million. Then the IRS criminal investigation agency was also involved with the bribery of $2.5

million. In total, there was between $8-$10 million given to keep things quiet.

Family Drama

In challenging times, friends and family are supposed to be our support system. It's them whom we can fall back on and rely on for protection and welfare. Unfortunately, our case was entirely the opposite. My aunts and uncles breached all boundaries of decency, as their desperation to get easy money turned them into devils.

* * *

Once they found that my father had that type of money, they began gang-stalking us. In other words, there were groups of people who would follow us around, watch us, and harass us in different ways. The ultimate goal was intimidation, and it was not just by people we didn't know. My father's sisters, Mevlina and Margie Jones, had moved into the neighbor's house, which was about three houses down from our house on Carolina Avenue. They were there to watch us come and go. They tried to set us up for robbery and for kidnapping by studying our movements. They found out how much money my dad had, and they wanted it by any means.

They offered candy to my sister and me, then they told us that our parents had asked them to pick us up. They had come to pick us up in a white van. Once we got in, the van got moving until it reached its destination, which was a house across the street from our house. If I remember right, it seemed to be the same house that my father paid for his illegitimate daughters to live in. My father's illegitimate daughter's name was Angie Williams Yarborough. My father had been taking care of her ever since we moved here. He actually brought her with us from somewhere near Chicago.

My father's sisters and brothers took us to the apartment that I thought was downstairs or next to that apartment. It was a duplex, from what I faintly remember. We were being held across the street from our own house. They were very abusive toward us and didn't give us anything to eat the entire day.

My father's sister Margie Jones was involved in the kidnapping. Now, my aunt knew that my father had put money in child trust accounts for my sister and me. He had done so because everything seemed uncertain, and he wanted to secure our future in any way that he could. Of course, she did not reveal her identity and spoke in a made-up voice when she called my father and asked him for the ransom. They demanded $500,000. He had put $250,000 in each of my sisters' accounts and locked another $300,000 for me.

My mom agreed to pay the money, only if she proved that we were in her possession. My aunt handed me the phone, and from my voice, Mom identified right away who it was. She then spoke to my sister, who pleaded for help. I was five years old at that time, while my sister was older.

What happened next ran chills down my spine. The telephone was in the living room, which was where we sat with my aunt as she spoke with my mother on the phone. My uncle came into the living room, grabbed my sister by the arm, and dragged her to the bedroom. He left the door open for me to see his craziness. He threw my sister on the bed and began raping her. I couldn't believe he was such a monster. My sister kept on screaming and pleading, but that miserable man showed no mercy. My mother on the other side of the phone could hear my sister's screams, but she didn't know the reason behind the pain.

She was screaming at the top of her lungs. My mother could hear her cries, and she asked me what was happening in the background. I couldn't answer. My mom demanded that she let go of her youngest son first, which was me. All she heard was my sister screaming for help. She said she would give half the money if they let me go.

They—my mother, father, and FBI agents--loaded a briefcase with all the cash. Later, I was told that my dad reversed the money from my sisters' accounts to pay for the ransom. He couldn't take any money from my account because I needed to be 21 for that money to be redeemed. Aunt Margie was the one who made the call. She asked the money to be sent with Derek, who was Dad's brother, but my mom sent Louise with him, who was her brother.

They released me first as my mom had asked them too, since I was the younger one. I really wished they had let my sister go first because they were treating her very wrong.

Once Margie received the remaining amount of money, she let go of my sister. I remember my mother telling my father that the money was taken out of my sister's trust funds. The two of my sisters had $250,000 each, which was a total of 500,000. My mother had taken that money out of their trust funds in order to free my sister and me from the kidnapping.

I was five years old, so the money in my trust account couldn't be withdrawn. The Bank of America had its policies and ways of protecting minors from being defrauded. That was how the money in my trust account was safe. The kidnapping wasn't a sudden incident but well-planned. We were watched for months before being kidnapped. I don't know if my Aunt Regina had anything to do with it, but I kind of think she was involved in it one way or another.

* * *

My Aunt Regina wanted more money, and she was willing to do anything for it. One day, as mom and dad left the house, she, along with her husband, sneaked in. They knew where my parents hid the spare key, so breaking in wasn't that big of a challenge for them. She ransacked my parents' room and their bed. It was under the mattress where she found around a million dollars that she filled in trash bags to take along with her.

The trash bags were full till the top. I was five years old at the time. It was my dad's earnings from the tour concert, but little did he know that the money wasn't safe in the house. She even took my mom's diamond rings and other valuable jewelry without any shame. She wasn't there for the money, though. She was there for the trust fund documents in the name of my sister, and she found them as well.

Upon finding the documents, she got with someone on the phone who was guiding her as to how the documents were to be modified to benefit her. Yes, it was Marshall Thompson on the line as she had to come into the hallway of the living room since it was where the phone was. He then asked her to change my mother's name and write hers instead. She had brought tapes and white-out with her, so finding the documents wasn't a surprise, but she was looking for them. She then had me remove my father's name so that she could put Marshall Thompsons' name there in place of Dad's.

She took the money, the jewelry, and the child trust account documents with her. Again, it was all happening in 1983, and the world wasn't digital, hence such tampering was possible. When my mom returned home, I told her that Aunt Regina was here. She confronted her, but she outright denied it, so there wasn't much Mom could do. She just stopped talking to her. A few years passed without her speaking to Aunt Regina.

However, after the documents of the trust fund accounts went missing, my mother lost all her trust in Aunt Regina. She went as far as going to the police department to file a report. She had a police report written against her sister at the St. Louis Police Department, Missouri.

It was around 1981. She reported that her sister stole the trust account documents and was involved in forgery and fraud. The police only registered her complaint but took no action. It was because they didn't find enough evidence to prosecute her.

The documentation of the bank had evidential proof, but for some reason, they weren't able to recover it. I still think she did not prosecute her fully because my aunt threatened that if she did, she would tell the police that she was the one who allowed my aunt to drown me. So in such a situation, she would have been incriminated by allowing her own sister to drown her own son in front of her.

It was terrible to grow up around people who cared for nothing but money. My dad probably made some wrong choices along the way that led our lives into such complexities. Regardless, we as children never deserved to be abused, harassed, and tortured for materialistic gains. I know my father was a good man, but what happened to him wasn't good in any regard.

My childhood was traumatic and disturbing, but I managed to fight my way through. I know I wouldn't have survived all the pain and fear if it wasn't for a specific purpose.

* * *

My father's siblings could not handle my father's fame and fortune. My maternal aunts and uncles weren't a lot different, either. They were envious of my mother's stable life but never showed it, not unless they found an opportunity to take advantage of the situation to their benefit.

Mom's sister, Regina Cheryl Dixon, wanted to make money, and she was willing to go to all extents to achieve what she wanted. My relatives didn't care about the kind of situation we were in or the challenges we were facing on a day-to-day basis, especially after the corruption within the record label. It caused us to be in a state of poverty and destitution, but nobody cared. Like vultures who show no mercy to their prey, my relatives were inconsiderate of our problems.

* * *

After my father returned from the tour with the Chi-Lites, his siblings began asking him for money. Now his sister and brother were already involved in organized crime and criminal activity. His brother's name was Ken Jones, and he was a member of organized crime in St. Louis. He hijacked 18-wheeler trucks for the mob and sold all of the merchandise. The mob would sell that merchandise to small vendors and stores. In return, of course, he received payment. My father's sister, on the other hand, was involved in narcotics and drug dealing.

Unfortunately, my aunt and uncles worked for the same mob as the record company, and they were more focused on proving their loyalty to the criminals than they were concerned for my father's wellbeing. My dad's sister even paid one of our neighbors to cut our brake lines in order to nearly kill us so that he wouldn't be able to testify against them.

Marshall Thompson, through his corruption, defrauded my father, which was why Dad couldn't receive his royalties or any part of the revenues. Later, Marshall wanted to steal all the funds that my father had put up in the trust accounts.

Money Is The Root Of All Evil

More and more drama continued, proving that money truly was the root of all evil. My Aunt Regina had become ruthless, and she went as far as trying to take my life. My aunt drowned me in a tub filled with water. I was there with my sister Janelle, who was only a year older. She tried to save me, but she was young and weak. So, my aunt slammed her into the wall and broke her nose. Then, my aunt continued to keep me drowned until I passed away. She succeeded, but only for a short while.

My heart stopped beating, and I lay lifeless when the EMTs were called. I was resuscitated after about maybe about three and a half minutes. Yes, I had died for a few minutes from drowning. Two EMTs had arrived. One of them was a Caucasian man, and the other was an African American woman. I was later told that the African American woman had declared me dead after trying for a minute. She was discouraging the Caucasian man from trying to save me because she felt it wasn't going to bring back a dead kid, but God had different plans.

However, the Caucasian EMT said that he couldn't let a five-year-old die. He said I had my whole life ahead of me, and I deserved to live. It took him four long minutes, but he resuscitated me. The EMT workers were told that I had "accidentally" drowned. I was rushed to the children's hospital, which was located almost seven blocks away from where we lived. I went through recovery and dealt with the trauma. The next few years were spent in peace. I did survive that day but ended up getting amnesia. I failed to remember most of what happened around me, and it remained that way until I turned 30 years old. That was when my memory began returning.

***

At one point, the police reached out to my mother, telling her that her brother had been found dead in the Merrimack River while he was on a boating trip with her sister Regina. They were not sure whether it should be treated as a homicide. She was told that he was found with his skull fractured, bruised, and broken, and they were still conducting their investigation. My mother started going into hysterics, thinking her sister Regina, along with dad's siblings, had set up her brother and murdered him.

She thought of all the different scenarios. One of them was thinking that maybe Regina had hired a hitman and got him drunk. Then, he bashed her brother in the head and was thrown off the boat.

My uncle was very protective of my mother, and he would never let his sister be exploited. He was very protective and made sure that no one would ever doing anything to her. So, my mother kind of thought that they wanted to get him out of the way so that they would be able to control and exploit her better. He had even found out that Regina had sold those trust documents and tried to get those trust documents back from her. According to the police, this may also have played a role in them wanting him dead.

So, Regina wanted a hitman to take my father's brother's life. She thought that if her brother had died, my dad's brother needed to die too. The next day, they found my dad's brother dead in his backyard, shot in the back of his head. God knows if it was her, or something else, but the only thing for sure is that Uncle Cookie lost his life.

* * *

As you can see, our life—especially my father's—was in no way calm or under control. He was battling with life and death situations on a regular basis, and it was coming from people whom he called family.

My father cooperated with Marshall as much as he could, but

despite that, Marshall always envied him. He even went so far as to instruct my aunts and uncles to drug my dad with food and drinks. They'd offer my dad drinks when he returned from concerts, overdosing him with different substances such as LSD and PCP.

Aunt Regina and my mother would call the local ambulance to come out and put him in the psych ward division of the Barnes and Jewish Hospital and also Malcolm Bliss Hospital, pretending like he went into a schizophrenic episode.

Each time they gave him the drinks, he'd overdose and be rushed to the hospital. They'd only take him to a couple of hospitals, where Marshall had bribed the doctors to declare him schizophrenic. Of course, the doctors were never going to be honest, since they were receiving stacks of cash in a brown paper bag in excess of I believe $50,000. Marshall had handed the bag of money to one of the doctors, saying that he wanted my dad to be declared schizophrenic. He was perfectly fine, and it was the LSD and PCP that made him unwell. Since the doctors never revealed that, no one found out.

The LSD dose was given to my father by Aunt Regina. Sometimes, she would even pay $500 to my sister Tammico to do it. Since my eldest sister had a bond with my aunt, she ended up doing it. Tranelle and I had witnessed Regina using the three-inch bottle being mixed in his drink, and we informed Mom right away. Mom believed us and went as far as filing a report. When the police questioned her, she outright denied, and since no one had any evidence, she was released.

Even though my father had no beef against anyone, everyone wanted to take advantage of him. He suffered in various ways, but not once were his sacrifices acknowledged. His life was difficult, particularly toward the end, but no one stayed by his side. The only people who wished well for him were his children, but the events of his life had changed him a great deal, and he was no longer the person he once was.

I even saw father once crying profusely. He was drained and tired of defending himself. He was displeased with how my mother, her siblings, and his siblings had all joined hands against him under Marshall Thompson. It was very unfair to him, to say the least. He was forcefully confined in the mental ward and given shots for treatment of a disease he had never had.

* * *

In the midst of the chaos, time continued to progress, and I turned nine years old. My mom and dad had separated, so my mom was trying to raise us on her own. She had refused to take any money from my father, so she was solely responsible for the finances. Not having a lot of options and fighting poverty, my mom finally spoke to Aunt Regina for help.

My aunt advised my mother to poison me. The deal was that my mother couldn't access the funds in the accounts unless I had an accidental death or by declaring me mentally unstable. Since I was nine, declaring myself mentally unstable was out of the question. So, she had talked my mother and Tameko into using arsenic poisoning, suggesting they place it in the oatmeal dish that they was feeding me. Within four days, there were dark circles under my eyes, and my sides and my stomach began to hurt constantly. I was enrolled in a school in St. Louis, Missouri, and I went to the nurse and told her how I had been feeling.

The nurse called my mother, and I was taken to the hospital, which was where I was put on a dialysis machine because my kidney had gone into failure. The blood toxicology report showed that I had arsenic and rat poison in my blood. There was rat poison in my food, making this another yet another attempt that my aunt and mother took at ending my life.

The doctors asked my mother how rat poison got into my blood stream, upon which Mom told them that I had mistakenly eaten mothballs for candies. She even told me to say this to the doctors if asked. I told her I hadn't done any such thing, but she said she'd get in trouble if I didn't say I had mistakenly eaten mothballs. I was too young to understand what she meant at that time, but now I know very well what had happened.

My kidney function had reduced to 5%, which was very alarming. I stayed in the children's hospital for the next six months or so. Through my kidney dialysis, they pumped out the poison, as well as pumped fluids in and out of my body since my kidney wasn't functioning. I did return to school during the time when my kidneys were being dialyzed. There was a surgical pump in my arm that I did not like because all the kids kept asking me about it. Hence, I had it placed in my legs instead. Fortunately, within a year, my kidney function got back to normal.

* * *

The idea of trying to take my life to get trust fund money wasn't new. One time, I was asked to fake my death by going to a funeral home at the age of about six years old. I was asked to lay in a casket and be very still while I was injected with a substance that prevented my movement and caused me to be temporarily paralyzed. I believe this was used as an attempt to get access to my Bank of America Trust Fund and Life Insurance Benefits. Shortly afterward, my first name was changed from Creadel to Darren. To this day, I don't understand why my name was then changed in 1982 from my father's first name Creadel to Darren.

Gang Activity & Intimidation

As I mentioned before, the purpose of the involvement of the FBI and the IRS was because they were closely monitoring the activities of the DeCalavantee family. They were an Italian American organized crime (mafia) family in New Jersey that started as early as the first part of the 19th century. Initially, they only functioned in central New Jersey and New York. Gradually, their network spread, and they made connections and allies that were associated with the Philadelphia crime family.

The family worked with Brunswick Records through its owner Nate. In turn, they basically got involved with the record label by financing the record company. First, they financed some record contracts with Jackie Wilson, one of the major artists of the record label. They also started paying for his promotional activities.

Jackie Wilson was a Brunswick Records musician who the FBI asked to give testimony against Brunswick Records concerning the mafia involvement in helping operations of the label. He was told by the Jersey Crime Mafia boss, Simon DeCavalcante, and Chicago and New York crime family to fake a stroke in order to prevent the mafia from being investigated by the FBI and IRS Criminal Investigations.

So, on September 29, 1975, Jackie was one of the featured acts in Dick Clark's Good Ol' Rock and Roll Revue, hosted by the Latin Casino in Cherry Hill, New Jersey. He was in the middle of singing "Lonely Teardrops" when he allegedly suffered a massive heart attack.

I recall visiting Jackie with my father, mother, and the other Chi-Lites members, and I saw him sitting in a chair with his legs crossed while he casually talked on the phone, playing cards at his table.

Then I remember Jackie getting up to play music while laughing with my father and the other Chi-Lites musicians. He laughed and joked about his fake stroke that he allegedly had in order to prevent FBI investigations, then excessively flirted with my mother, asking her to dance with him. In addition to my father, mother, and the Chi-Lites, musician, Nat Tranopol was also there.

After a few more conversations and important meetings involving Brunswick Records executives and Mafia Boss Simon Decavalantee and FBI discussions plans, we went back to our homes. Then, they began to do the same with the management of the Chi-Lites. They basically helped market the band, as well as pay for their concerts, instruments, and various concert promotions. The IRS got aware of the Decalavantee family financing the Chi-Lites campaign.

* * *

Again, the leader of the crime family that I met was named Simon Decavalantee. He was the one who was directly dealing with the Chi-Lites. You may be wondering why they financed the bands and artists and what they got out of it. The answer to it is simple. They used musicians to smuggle narcotics in and out of the United States of America. So yes, the Chi-Lites also helped them smuggle and traffic drugs and money in and out of the country. Mainly, it was Nate's involvement, but as time progressed, everyone associated with the band was part of the crime in one way or the other. All of it was done in return to get financed for their concerts and filling their pockets with decent money.

Besides paying for their travel and tour expenses, the Decavalantees also paid for promotional concerts in Las Vegas and other major venues. They also helped the band make its way into certain casinos throughout the country, as well as perform abroad. In exchange, the Chi-Lites had to traffic drugs for them. This activity was heavily encouraged by Marshall Thompson.

In addition to being a band member, Marshall was a police officer who used his credentials and accessibility to steal police badges from the police department. He stole thousands and thousands of badges from the Dixon Police Department of Illinois and gave them to the members of the mafia. They then used these badges to smuggle drugs throughout the country. All those badges were used for illegal drug seizures by powerful drug dealers throughout Chicago, New Jersey, St. Louis, and Missouri.

Of course, the drugs were illegally confiscated and sold with the help of the stolen police badges that Marshall provided. Marshall had proved his loyalty to the Decavalantee family in various ways. In any way that he could, he facilitated them to sell drugs and generate insane amounts of money.

He even was once part of a shootout, so the family trusted him. After the shootout, he came to our door. His shirt was covered in blood, and he was crying like a child who was scared and regretful about what he had done. He was still new to everything, and he told my father and mother while profusely crying that a drug deal had gone wrong, and he had no other option but to use his gun to protect himself. As a result, he ended up killing three guys.

He wasn't just there to share his regret or ease his pain. He was there because he wanted my mom and dad to help him get his heroin. He was a heroin addict, and he believed the only way he could calm himself was by taking a dose. He was dressed in a neat suit that was covered in blood. That was the only time I saw him so weak. That's what drugs probably do to you, and then karma has its own way of showing up.

* * *

I'm not just conveying drug trafficking stories that I heard about. I literally witnessed the exchanges and stacks of army duffel bags full of money, cocaine, and heroin. There was a point when things in the city weren't exactly under control; drugs and crime were at all-time high. It was around that time that Marshall asked Mom and Dad to hide some stash in her house. The stash wasn't just a few grams; it was over 2,000 kilos.

My dad used the kitchen cabinets to store the drugs. At one point, every cabinet in the kitchen had nothing but cocaine and heroin in it. Even the refrigerator was used as a storage facility. The drugs were so much in the quantity that even after stacking up every part of the kitchen, he still couldn't hide all of it. Naturally, he had to look for other options. He used our closet, took out our clothes, and stuffed it with packs of drugs. I'm not sure how or why my father's business partner got involved in the drug business. But like they say, it's far easier to get in than it is to get out.

On another occasion, he got his hands on stolen U.S. treasury notes in order to create phony money. He even brought lots of counterfeit bills to our house and gave them to my father. Dad found a spot in the house and stored the notes there. Millions of dollars were printed illegally to be sold for $300,000 in real money.

For obvious reasons, the Decavalantee family became very interested in the stolen notes of the US treasury. So, besides drugs, Marshall was getting involved in all kinds of illegal activities. Since he was a drug addict, he never got an opportunity to sit down and realize what he was getting himself into. Consequently, we were also sharing the risks without sharing the benefits.

* * *

On another occasion, I saw Simon come over to our house with a friend. His friend's name was Gaetano Vastola, but he was referring to him as Sunny. It turned out that Sunny was a captain of the mob that worked for the Decavalantee family. My father wasn't home, so my mom had to deal with the two of them.

I don't know exactly how or why they had to act so inhumanly that they took advantage of my father's absence and laid hands on my mother. He raped her mercilessly, knowing we, the kids, were home. They didn't care about the trauma that we had to deal with and didn't lose an opportunity to bring out the animal that was hiding inside them. They had a gun on my sister and me, and they told her that if she did not do as she was told, they would kill us. She was taken to the back bedroom, and it was where they raped her.

When Dad got back, he was furious. He couldn't take the news and immediately set off to confront Sonny. He found him and they got into a fistfight. Dad punched his face numerous times, and one of the blows got Sonny's nose. Although he had the satisfaction of breaking Sonny's nose, Dad was still very disturbed about what had happened.

As was expected, the mafia sent a few goons to take revenge. They drove up in a black limousine, forced their way into our house, and asked Dad to come with them. At first, my father didn't agree, but after giving it some thought, he figured it was best for him to leave. He realized that he could be murdered as the people he was dealing with were extremely dangerous. Plus, he didn't want to drag us into these complex problems. He kissed my sisters and me then got into the black limousine and drove away.

He returned a few hours later with a broken hand that was covered with a sling and a cast.

* * *

Once Dad was the target of the hitman, and I'm not sure how Mom knew. I'm not saying she hired the hitman, but she somehow knew there was a man across the street on top of the roof, pointing a gun at him. She told Dad to get out of the way, and he jumped immediately. Three bullets hit the wall, barely missing him. Had he not moved, the bullet would have ended his life. There were three shots that came through the window. Two of the shots were aimed at his head, and one shot was aimed at his chest.

When the police came by the house, they actually did a crime scene investigation. They determined that the bullets had entered from the window from the rooftop across the house. The actual hitman who tried to shoot him was on top of the roof of that apartment complex. The very same apartment complex that my father's illegitimate daughter and her grandmother lived in was right in front of the house. Coincidence or is there something deeper going on that we didn't know about...?

Royalty Theft

After the death of my father, we strongly believed that the primary reason for his homelessness was that the royalties had not been paid by Brunswick Records. It was only after his death that Marshall contacted my mom on behalf of Brunswick Records, pretending they were willing to pay royalties after his death to avoid a lawsuit from my mother.

His lawyer said that he had settled for $100,000 to get the royalties as backed royalties since 1968-1994. In 1994, my mother then signed a new contract that stated we would receive 25% of royalties, twice a year. My mom started receiving royalty checks, which began with only $150. This money supposedly represented the MC Hammer remake, including all 18 records that were previously recorded by my father and the Chi-Lites. I suggested that my mother contact the FBI and local news outlets, including NBC, FOX, and Warner Brothers St. Louis News Network, which was very prevalent at the time.

After the FBI was contacted, the corrupt record label of Brunswick Records quickly sent a $2,500 check in the mail the next day. With sales statements that reported over 10 million records sold for the quarter, the $2,500 was supposed to be a representation of the royalty amount that was owed.

The following information was provided by https://www.whosampled.com/Chi-Lites/

- 123 samples, 50 covers
- Are You My Woman? (Tell Me So)(1970) was sampled in Crazy in Love by Beyoncé feat. Jay Z(2003)
- #1 With a Bullet by Kool G Rap & DJ Polo feat. Big Kane (1992)
- Emotional by Saweetie and Quavo(2019)see six more connections

Inside the Chi-Lites Music

- That's How Long(1974) was sampled in December 4 by Jay-Z (2003)
- V.S.O.P. by K. Michelle (2013)
- Prelude by Duke Dumont (2009)
- "Have You Seen Her" (1971) was sampled in Letter to P by Havoc (2009)
- "Dollar and a Dream" by The Game feat. Ab-Soul (2015)
- "Who Stole the Soul?" by Public Enemy(1990) see 26 more connections
- "Oh Girl" (1972) was sampled in "Girl" by Paul Wall (2005)
- "Dans Ma Ruche" by Guizmo (2014) was covered in
- "Oh Girl" by Young-Holt
- "Unlimited" (1972) see 14 more connections
- "My First Mistake" (1977) was sampled in "Needin' U" by David
- "Morales" (1998)
- "No Mistakes" by DJ
- "Duke" (1996)
- "First Love" by John
- "Julius" Knight (2000) Chi-Lites Group Members: Eugene Record, Clarence Johnson, Anthony Watson, Creadel Jones, Danny Johnson Marshall, Thompson, Robert Lester, Ronald Scott, Stanley Anderson

Upon finding out about the different places the Chi-Lites music was being used, I told my mom that we needed to start an investigation with the FBI for royalty theft on Marshall Thompson's part. She agreed and soon, we started an investigation of my dad's case. Virgil Johnson was the FBI agent we talked to in St. Louis, Missouri, and after we told him about the facts, Marshall Thompson was shortly investigated and arrested by the IRS. Allegedly, he had been found to be active in different illegal activities.

Marshall not only committed royalty theft but was also responsible for illegally selling police badges upon an investigation conducted. Additionally, the IRS started investigating him from 2001-2005, discovering that he did commit tax evasion and money laundering. Therefore, they eventually froze his bank account.

In 2005, as a reward for providing them with the information about Marshall, the IRS gave me a $7,500 check. I immediately deposited it to Bank of America to open a bank account and was told that I already had a trust fund account which had been accumulating since 1985. It shook me up, for the same money I thought Aunt Regina had stolen was still there and was now worth $875,000.

Essentially, the successful investigation that led to Marshall's bank and trust fund accounts to be frozen by the IRS made him no longer have control over my trust funds. It's amazing how life works for I was just homeless awhile back in California due to financial troubles.

* * *

My mom's death was shortly followed by me traveling to New York to visit the owner of Brunswick Records, Paul Tarnopol. Paul was responsible for not paying the royalties of my father, and he had cheated us by selling the Chi-Lites catalog to various artists without paying us even a fraction in royalties.

When I went to Paul's office in New York, I asked the security guard, "What floor is Paul Tarnopol's office?" After he directed me to the correct place, I could hear people talking about me through the doors saying, "Creadel Jones' son is here! What do we do?"

Paul replied, "Don't let him come in. Run out of the office."

I tried to open the door to Paul's office, but unfortunately, it was locked. I called on the speaker phone, asking to unlock the door but received no response. I proceeded to the elevator again, and I saw 3-4 Mexican men and a bodyguard that was about 6'5 coming from the office right next to the Brunswick Records office. Right when I was walking into the elevator, another 6'5 white man wearing a London fall trench coat followed me until I went inside.

I felt as if I was being indirectly forced out of the premises. I wasn't going to leave Paul Tarnopol without talking to him. So, the next day, I came back to the office again and finally met him. I asked him about what happened the previous day, to which he replied, "I didn't do anything!"

I proceeded to tell him about my financial situation and how I was living in a shelter as I couldn't afford to live anywhere else. Paul suggested that he'd drop me off at the shelter and gave me $100, which was disappointing, to say the least. This conversation led to another $25 million lawsuit filed on Brunswick Records.

Because of the difficulties we had faced abruptly, we required finances to survive as we had been indirectly cheated by Jay-Z and Beyonce for the two songs they remade. My sisters and I took a collateral loan, and I talked to Paul again, this time demanding our royalties immediately as we couldn't arrange a funeral for our mother. Paul told us he'd send us $10,000 through Western Union. However, he only sent $2,600 like he would each time we demanded our royalties.

I went to the FBI office in St. Louis, Missouri, to report Brunswick Records, and surprisingly, they told me I had a pending case of disturbing the peace. The FBI then held me 'til they sent me over to the St. Ann police department the next month. Nobody helped me or bailed me out of jail during my period there, and as I came out of jail, I couldn't find my car that my mother had given to me.

I found out that my sister had stolen my car, and the furniture in my apartment was also missing. I asked the landlord what had happened, and he told me that it was sent out of the apartment as they had no idea how long it would take for me to be back from jail. So, they emptied the space.

The Business Proposal/ Celebrity Run-Ins

I approached various celebrities with a business proposal to sell the Chi-Lites catalog, namely, Bill Cosby, Whoopi Goldberg, B.B King, Dianna Ross, Russel Simmons, and more. Unfortunately, most of them refused the offer until one day, I was at Russel Simmons' record label company, and shortly afterward, I saw Jay-Z walking into the room.

Someone had previously suggested I discuss the business proposal with Jay-Z, and although I was hesitant at first, I reached out to him and told him about the business plan. He was interested in buying the Chi-Lites' catalog, and it was a great offer, so I asked my mom, "Why don't we just sell the royalty catalog that we have instead of trying to go back and forth to the FBI?" She agreed, and I told Jay-Z that I would send him the attorney's number, my number, and all details of the record.

After sending him the details and the entire business plan, he agreed to buy two songs of the Chi-Lites, "Got Me Going So Crazy Right Now" and "That's How Long," which were both remade by him and his wife.

I asked my mom how much we should sell those royalties for, and I suggested we ask for a million dollars to which she refused because she believed they wouldn't pay that much. She suggested we ask for $375,000 instead.

I was hesitant at first but later agreed to sell those songs for $375,000. However, Jay-Z was persuaded to pay the money to Brunswick Records for two singles instead of the entire catalog, and we never received a dime out of those singles. I felt disappointed and cheated again.

Soon, my mother died in 2005, and my sisters and I had very little finances to arrange for her funeral. We felt completely hopeless. Throughout my involvement with the investigation of the corruption and exploitation of my father's music legacy with

Inside the Chi-Lites Music

the Chi-Lites, I have had my fair attempts at acquiring celebrity assistance involving the investigation of my father's death.

Oprah Winfrey, Gayle King, Al Sharpton, Whoopi Goldberg, William Cosby, Evander Holyfield, Francis C. Wesling, Neil Fuller, Professor Griff, and many others were who I had directly contacted in order to acquire proper private investigations into the death of my father.

Despite my attempts to obtain cooperation from Oprah Winfrey and the celebrities mentioned throughout this story, I have yet to see any cooperation from any of these fellow black celebrities.

No complete FBI investigation and private investigators have offered their aid or assistance in this ongoing story. Investigations are needed. Our story is still left lacking full investigation by both the FBI and Hollywood entertainment industry.

After going to Bill Cosby's home, speaking with Gayle King and her staff at O magazine, and speaking to the vice president of Harpo Studios for over seven years, everyone has failed and refused to review, investigate, assist, or cover any story details pertaining to the death of my father or my mother who died mysteriously after being left in a coma for over two months.

* * *

On one occasion, I had contacted Gayle King office in New York, only to be threatened by her staff that if I was to continue to try to contact Gayle King and her office, they were going to physically attack me and contact the police.

Her office manager even threatened to kill me, further stating that he would come to my home if he had to and kill me if I continue to call Gayle King's office in New York at O magazine.

Despite the fact that Oprah Winfrey could have easily resolved this by doing an investigational exclusive, she continued to help cover up the whole entire story, even going as far as to have me arrested after I demonstrated in front of Harpo Studio located in Chicago, Illinois.

* * *

I can recall talking to Sheri Salata, the former senior executive producer of the Oprah Winfrey Show, on a weekly basis in order to have a media investigation involving the death of my father and the exploitation of the Chi-Lites music.

I even offered an idea for Oprah Winfrey to create a celebrity inner city program in which I called O Ambassadors. I used the letter 'O' as the first initial in front of the word ambassadors to signify the connection to Oprah Winfrey. This program I created meant to enact a highly skilled trade apprenticeship program, which would incorporate on-the-job training in fields that will help third-world countries and impoverished areas rebuild their communities.

By allowing troubled youth and inner-city at-risk individuals to travel abroad to different third-world countries, they would be able to help rebuild their communities and empower villages and cities.

These at-risk youth would have had the ability to learn skilled trades and certified training from qualified, licensed educated professionals who were willing to train these inner cities to help change their lives.

This program also would have allowed at-risk and impoverished individuals to travel abroad, allow a rewarding lifetime experience to help shape character, and offer an opportunity to engage in constructive multicultural experiences.

After offering the idea of O-Ambassadors to Sheri Salata, I was greeted with immediate interest and excited anticipation and co-operation from Sheri. She then told me to send the written project pitch directly by her email. In which she provided to me. I was to later find out that Sheri had used and stolen the idea then giving it to a Caucasian man who appeared on the Oprah Winfrey show, then pretended as if he created the O-Ambassadors program, I created and developed for Oprah Winfrey and Sheri Salata.

I felt betrayed. How could the executive producer steal the very program that I decided to create in order to help inner city at-risk African-American youth and young adults throughout inner cities in the United States? I wanted to confront her. As I was coming out of church, I saw Sheri walking in downtown Detroit, Michigan. I called her name, and she began running as fast as she could down the street.

I was shocked and amazed; I couldn't understand what in the hell was going on. She continued to run as fast as she could, which wasn't that fast because she's a slightly overweight woman. I tried to contact her on her website, phone, and email, but she refused to return any calls. This was just one of many exploitations I faced while attempting to acquire celebrity assistance.

Another such occasion occurred with Janet Jackson. After attempting to go to the Jackson Family Havenhurst mansion in Encino, California, I was greeted by one of the security managers who happened to be the nephew of Malcolm X.

I had typed up a letter in which I had expected to present to Catherine Jackson, which included full details involving the exploitation of my father, my family, and the Chi-Lites. I was informed by the security manager that the Jacksons were trying to sell the home.

He told me that Latoya Jackson and the Jackson Family frequently came to the home, further stating that he would give the letter directly to them on their next visit. I said thank you and proceeded to go. As I walked out of the driveway, I saw a black SUV pull up and quickly back out of the driveway.

Not knowing whether this was Katherine Jackson, Latoya Jackson, or the children of Michael Jackson, I continued to proceed to the bus stop. While I waited for the bus, I noticed the same black SUV pulling up to the curb at the corner. A black lady walkout of the SUV and just stared at me.

This lady seemed to stare until the bus arrived. Then, the lady began to follow behind me and walk on the bus. I was unaware that this lady was Janet Jackson, and I gave her a compliment about how beautiful she was.

Suddenly, Janet began to go on a tantrum, stating, "He can't say that to me! He can't say that to me!" She then demanded that the bus driver pull over the bus immediately.

Her own driver with the company here on the bus and security tried to tell her, "He's just complimenting you." However, Janet Jackson wasn't having any of that. I couldn't believe that this is the attitude that I received from the Jackson family.

Not to mention, I had a Facebook conversation with BG (Blanket) Jackson, Michael Jackson's youngest son about my family's struggles. He said, "I don't care what happens to any other celebrities other than Whitney Houston. If you need any help; I don't do that. I don't care what happens to any black celebrities other than Whitney Houston."

I began to tell him how my father and the Chi-Lites helped Michael Jackson and the rest of the Jackson 5 get into the music industry by allowing the Jackson 5 to open up for the Chi-Lites.

His reply was that just because his father is a billionaire, that didn't mean he had to help anyone. All of this evidence still resulted in no action. The lack of FBI investigational support is noted and wills more suspicion involving the corruption of the FBI and its lack of investigative inquiry aid or assistance involving the death and financial abuse of my father and my mother.

A full investigation is needed. Overall, most of the celebrities declined my offer or ignored it completely.

A Cry for Help

Abuse and trauma weaken a person and make them lose hope. It can hurt us to the core and make us question our existence. Not every abuse and trauma leaves scars that require a lifetime to heal, but the ones that do make it very difficult to trod along the journey called life.

My family was abused by the hands of Marshall Thompson, our relatives, and Brunswick Records. We faced both financial and emotional turmoil. Our family suffered exploitation, which devasted my father's career and made him spend the last years of his life in severe depression and homelessness. What hurt him the most was to see his siblings poison him and drug him for financial gain. Even his wife had switched sides, and he was left on his own to fight the world.

Marshall Thompson was the main culprit and contributor along with Brunswick Records executives, and Nat Tarnopol. They were the main contributors to my father's declining health. She married my father in 1978 and remain married until his death on August 25th, 1994. My mother also worked as a stand-up comedian and a radio talk show host before completing her degree at Forest Park College.

* * *

Some of my parents' colleagues who often visited us were Michael Jackson, Whitney Houston, Chaka Khan, Katt Williams, Bernie Mac, Wanda Sykes, Prince, DMX, Kanye West and his mother, Robert Townsend, Martin Sheen, Charlie Sheen and the Sheen family, George Clooney, Ozzy Osbourne and the Osborne Family, etc. I can recall a brief conversation we had with Evander Holyfield in which we deeply explained the exploitation that we had gone through following the death of my father. The conversation lead to Evander Holyfield promising his help with aiding in investigations.

Despite my mother mailing Holyfield original copies of music contracts and record sales sheets reporting over 100 million records from 1968-1995. This included over 40 major record labels Brunswick Records executives licensed to sell my father's and the Chi-Lite's music.

We never heard back from Holyfield nor his staff until my mother went to his company and demanded our paperwork be sent back to us. His response was that he couldn't help due to his funds being exhausted, despite having just earned over $65 million from the Mike Tyson Fight.

Brunswick Records, Marshall Thompson, the Decavalantee organized crime family, and several of my aunts and uncles were responsible for the decline and ultimate destruction of my father's musical career with the Chi-Lites music group. Not only did they destroy my father's career, but they were responsible for ending the career of others in the industry as well.

My mother, Deborah Jones, continued as much as she could to help provide for us by working as a certified nurse assistant, and later a teacher after her graduation from St. Louis College. I am proud of all that she did. The reason she didn't take child support was that she wanted to disassociate herself and us from the band and its stakeholders.

* * *

I remember seeing Kanye West and his mother at a tour home in St. Louis after my mother contacted their church to receive financial assistance. They were accompanied by Martian Sheehan and Charlie Sheehan's family. On one occasion, my mother contacted Katherine Jackson. It was after she had met them at the Barnes-Jewish Hospital, where Latoya had come in for mental health treatment. I was 17 years old at the time.

At that time, I was forced to be confined in the hospital to receive mental health treatment so that the child trust funds in the Bank of America were accessible. They made multiple attempts, but, fortunately, never succeeded. The funds were hidden until September 17th, 2005, which was a few years after the IRS activity where they conducted an investigation I opened about royalty, defrauded. It was after I had gone to New York. It was around that time that my mother had asked my help to gain royalties that were rightly ours.

When I started to look into my dad's work and the Chi-Lites record and music sales, I discovered that various artists used the Chi-Lites music to claim their fame. For instance, M.C. Hammer remade "Have You Seen Her" and sold over 10 million records in less than a month. Of course, it was a fraudulent sales sheet and not the truth. This made M.C. Hammer the first rapper to ever go diamond in the history of rap music. Others like Jay-Z and Beyonce also went on to re-record my father's music. "Are You My Woman?" was sampled in "Crazy in Love." This re-record hit by Beyonce sold over 19 million copies in the first two months and earned Beyonce her first ever double diamond record, outselling Michael Jackson.

Other re-record remakes were by UB40, Paul Young, Mary J. Blige, Public Enemy, Kool Mo Dee, Emmortail Techniques, Seal, Chingy, P Diddy, Fantasia, and Alicia Keys. Alicia Keys went on to re-record "You Don't Know My Name," which was a success in itself.

Entertainers Against Exploitation & Corruption

As I alluded to earlier, I filed a $25 million lawsuit against Brunswick Records executive Paul Tarnopol at the age of 21. However, I was unable to continue and had to drop the charges because of the lack of finances available for conducting the trials and attorney fees alone. I saw approximately 30-40 different record labels selling the Chi-Lites music, and I was only receiving a quarter in royalties of what they had been gaining. I knew that it was over $9-$10 million in sales being made within the year, and that's when I was ready to conduct investigations with the IRS.

I wound up going to New York to continue the investigation and assist the IRS in uncovering all the activities that had taken place. Furthermore, I looked forward to meeting different celebrities that could help with financial assistance and fees for attorneys and private investigators. What I wanted to do was start an agency that recovered stolen royalties from record labels and rightfully hand them over to artists. You could think of it as an asset recovery agency, and this business was to be named "Entertainers Against Exploitation & Corruption, which was founded in Missouri in 2005."

Following the death of my mother on August 24th, 2003, I was focused entirely on establishing Entertainers Against Exploitation and Corruption and saving the hard-earned wealth of artists from greedy record labels. I believed that the complexities in receiving royalties were unjust for artists, and things needed to change. The first campaign of mine started as a demonstration protest against Oprah Winfrey, as she barely considered our subject of exploitation of legendary black artists and lacked professionalism towards our sentiments.

Legendary black artists that generated billions in revenue were financially exploited by major record companies as a result of racism and corruption within the music industry. Similar to my father in the Chi-Lites case, the abuse eventually led to his homelessness and death. This happened after selling 100, million records worldwide, which was due to the unfair treatment of record labels and having his money stolen from him.

Because racism was prevalent in the era, most black artists had a similar fate, as the corrupt record companies would exploit them as much as possible and steal royalties. So, I was set on a mission to eliminate any possibilities of exploitation and corruption against artists while highlighting record companies such as Brunswick Records who were responsible for the death and financial abuse of many leading Hollywood icons such as; my father, Creadel Jones, and the Chi-Lites, Jackie Wilson, Little Richard, Billie Holiday, Ellard Fitzgerald, Louis Armstrong, Duke Ellington, and many more artists throughout music in the present day.

Although I was focused on this mission, we still required media coverage and publicity to spread our voices and end these unjustified acts. To have a greater reach, I approached Oprah Winfrey to aid and help in investigating the exploitation and financial abuse of our family legacy. I went to various offices and set meetings to discuss and have Oprah intervene in the case of our Chi-Lites family. However, with time, we realized that she was barely interested in our case.

She not only refused our case with unprofessionalism, but she also didn't assist in contacting the FBI or any federal agency to investigate the issue. Even Gayle King had informed Oprah about the level of abuse and exploitation under the hands of Marshall Thompson, Brunswick Records, and my Aunt Regina Cheryl Dickson. The abuse eventually led to homelessness and then the death of Creadel Jones, which was a tragic event to be marked in the history of black lives, which was unfortunately ignored by Oprah Winfrey entirely.

I decided to hold a protest against Oprah Winfrey and her studios on September 13th, 2004. This was the very same day Oprah had decided to gift cars to wealthy upper-class families that didn't even need them, and it was an eye-opener for my family and me to witness. It was a time of great difficulty for me, as I was already broke. I had to use up my last dollar to get to Oprah Winfrey's studio for the protest.

Upon arriving at her studio, I had signs titled "STOP LEGACY ABUSE AND EXPLOITATION TO BLACK ICONS" with pictures of my father and mother's face. As I went to the studio, I saw a white female on the driveway in a brand-new Mercedes Benz.

I got to hear that Oprah was giving these cars away. The woman that was present at the studio didn't even need them, and most of them already had exquisite cars in their garages. "I don't know, and I don't need it. I'll give it to my daughter then," I heard some woman say to another. "I have a new BMW convertible," said another. This was ironic for me to believe considering the fact that Oprah completely disregarded my case.

To demonstrate my frustration, I handcuffed myself to the doorknob to make it difficult for security to do anything. Oprah quickly sent her personal bodyguard Tommy to ask me what I was doing.

I replied, "I am the son of Creadel Jones from the Chi-Lites music group and founder of the organization Entertainers Against Exploitation, and I've come here to talk to Oprah Winfrey concerning the exploitation of my father in the hands of greedy record label executives, resulting in homelessness and eventually death."

The bodyguard told me to wait and began talking over a headset. He told Oprah about me and my cause and asked her what to do. She told Tommy to call the police and have me arrested for disturbing the peace. Shortly, the Chicago police department arrived at the area and came to investigate.

The captain of the police department had a discussion with me and asked me if my father was Creadel Jones. He also told me that he was aware of my father's death and supported the cause I was presenting. He said I was a brave man to be able to attempt this, but he emphasized that many people often try to demonstrate and protest against Oprah Winfrey. Usually, they never reach a positive outcome. The captain of the police department also agreed that Oprah Winfrey should help the Chi-Lites family and me with this case.

The man went on to tell me another story of a woman that came down to the Oprah Winfrey show and protested by sitting outside her studio. The lady claimed Oprah stole her cookbook recipe after she had sent it to her to receive some help in marketing. Furthermore, Oprah and her TV show producers took the cookbook recipe and gave it to their white male friend to write it and steal the entire book idea.

Hearing about this event changed my perspective on Oprah Winfrey entirely. I had a bad feeling about her already, but this amplified my negative emotions concerning her. The police captain checked back with Oprah Winfrey to ask her about what she wanted them to do. After a brief pause, the captain came back and told me he hated that he had to arrest , but he admired my courage and conviction. Jokingly, he said, "One thing is for sure, you got her attention." I was shortly taken down to the Chicago police station and released after a short period.

Unfortunately, contacting Oprah Winfrey and the IRS were both unsuccessful events trying to get the idea of Entertainers Against Exploitation to reach an audience. However, I created my own website for the idea, and I still run it but to properly sponsor my idea, I still require extensive funds and publicity.

Although the investigation of my case was ignored, I still continue to run fundraisers for the investigation of royalty theft, and investigations of Brunswick Records to eliminate any sort of exploitation that these greedy record label companies commit against entertainers.

Paternity Court TV

Before my mom died, a lady named Angie Yarbrough had just come into the picture after hearing about the royalties that were being paid on my late father's account and claimed that she was his illegitimate child. Jay Ross called me and told me about this woman requesting royalties for child support. We later came to realize that she was the same woman my dad had been supporting financially, along with her grandmother, sisters, and cousins. My mother used to use her to babysit us.

We paid all her dues along with a dedicated $40,000 in trust funds for taking good care of her, but she just wanted the extra money. My mother suggested that she have a DNA test to prove her indirect relation with my father, but unfortunately, Mom died shortly afterward. Along with Angie, my father's ex-wife nae Ruby Jones, and her children also got involved upon knowing of the royalties to be paid to him.

Being unsuccessful in attempts to receive celebrity assistance on my idea Entertainers Against Exploiters, I looked forward to taking Angie Yarborough to paternity court and finding out if she actually was eligible to receive the royalty she'd been asking for. I contacted Angie and told her about showing up on Paternity Court TV, and she was ready to start.

Still, she said, "What if you're not the child?" to which I laughed off because my mother had married my father, so I had absolutely no doubts about the fact that I was my dad's child. My mother had been married to my father since 1978. We were always recognized by major record labels, including Brunswick Records, as the family of Creadel Jones. There was never any question about our blood relation to him.

I also asked the son of my dad's ex-wife to be a part of paternity court. Angie had branded herself as demanding nothing more than being a part of the legacy of Creadel Jones and not because of the money or royalties. I knew this was a lie as she only came forward upon knowing of royalties being paid out on my father's account.

I had strongly believed that Angie wasn't my father's biological daughter and was just looking to get some money out of us. The last time I saw Angie was when I was about five years old. She used to be a babysitter that lived across our house, and if she had any link to our father, my mother or sister would've notified me in some way. I always felt suspicious about her, and after her appearance on the Paternity Court TV.

My mother and I had always believed that the main reason for Angie Yarborough's appearance in our lives was the result of our royalty theft case being publicized. We believed Angie was never a biological daughter of my father's and just wanted a portion of our royalties solely because of greed. It was because of our firm faith in Angie being a fraud and having no relation to our family that we proceeded to appear on the Paternity Court TV series to settle this dispute.

After I had contacted the show's producers for my appearance with Angie, I was invited for an interview. Angie's mother used to be a mistress of my father's, but they never had a child together. So, my mother and I were sure about her being my father's illegitimate daughter.

Shortly, I was contacted by the network to do an update interview. Apparently, the hosts and producers of the show seemed to have believed Angie Yarborough's side of the story and were constantly asking me about my biological link to Creadel Jones. I clarified to them that I was the person to contact them for the show to investigate Angie's relation to my father. My own blood relation to the family was never the issue.

The interview was not successful because the producers and hosts were being inconsiderate of my situation and mistreated me. I started having serious doubts about whether the show would be able to expose the actual story and the truth behind Angie's connection to my father. They asked me to show them proof of being the actual biological child of Creadel Jones as part of their investigation.

So, I showed them my parent's marriage license and certificates. Brunswick Records also recognized me as the beneficiary of Creadel Jones and rightful heir to receive all royalties. They also declared that I was the only son of Creadel Jones. Since my father died in 1994, I had been aiding my mother in all aspects related to receiving my father's royalties and all other critical legal procedures.

I also informed the show about the lawsuit in which I was found as the legitimate heir of my father's estate against Brunswick Records, which was later approved by the civil court of New York City and Manhattan. There was never any doubt about my own legitimate connection with Creadel Jones, but the television show's host was determined to identify a loophole in the story and dramatically create a twist for the public.

During the show, the producers and the host were being abusive toward me during the live broadcast, which resulted in me not appearing again and letting go of this idea altogether. Angie was accompanied by a nephew of my father's that had been claiming to be his son.

However, anyone could easily identify that the person looked much different from my father. He was also being used by my late father's sisters to gain a portion of the royalties. What Angie failed to mention was that she had gone to probate court in Chicago, Illinois, and filed an estate case before even coming on the Paternity Court show with Judge Lauren Lake or even knowing or finding out whether she was an illegitimate daughter. Her goal had been to get money and as much revenue as she could out of the whole story and event.

To my surprise, following the DNA tests, Angie Yarborough was found to be biologically an illegitimate daughter of my father's. Even then, she had no remorse or empathy for our father and the difficulties he had gone through. It was visible that she was primarily on the show to gain publicity and earn as much as she could from the opportunity.

It is my belief that Judge Lauren Lake, the Paternity Court TV show, and their producers deliberately deceived and intentionally misled both the fans of the Chi-Lites and fans of the show in order to gain views from our case. It was difficult for me to accept Angie Yarborough as a biological sister of mine, but from the DNA tests shown, it was, unfortunately, the truth. I felt that the show did not highlight any part of the difficulties our family had faced since the death of my father in 1994. From the royalty frauds to the death of my mother and myself living on the streets, there was no concern placed by Judge Lauren Lake on our family's issues.

Prior to coming on the show, I was told by the producers that I was not to talk about how my father died homeless due to poverty and exploitation brought on by Brunswick Records, the greed and corruption of Marshall Thompson, and the exploitation of my father Creadel Jones by his greedy relatives. I did not like the way I had been treated in the show while Angie Yarborough and the other man had been treated much better. I could sense bias in Judge Lauren Lake, which didn't work in my favor.

Inside the Chi-Lites Music

Run-In With Justin: Part 1

Eventually, over time things progressed to become more difficult in our lives. We were being gang stalked throughout several different states including California, New York, Ohio, Michigan, Missouri, Illinois, Arizona, and Texas. This was a complete nightmare. I was to be followed to every location that I went, including my college, stores, businesses, even outside of my home.

I started getting gang-stalked by my father's nephew, Justin Riveria. Justin started following me all the way to Detroit and to the Path of Life Ministries in California, where I met him. He looked suspicious, so I asked him if he knew my father.

He replied, "Yes, he's my uncle." I proceeded to ask him why he was there, which he didn't reply to. So, I asked him if he knew about my trust fund, and he replied, "Yes, your sister told me about it, but she is too afraid to get it out."

I wondered why she was afraid of taking it out because it was our money. Soon, Justin started gang-stalking me and harassing me into giving him the trust fund money, which made me understand the reason my sister was afraid to take it out. Eventually, it led to death threats.

* * *

Illegal surveillance became a norm for me. A while later, I got to find out cameras were installed throughout my home in Detroit and Flint, Michigan. I discovered these cameras after walking downstairs in my basement, where I noticed red recording lights illuminating my entire living room.

I quickly tried to look for the location of these cameras and noticed a wire leading from the outside of the door and extending outside of the exterior door. I quickly cut the wire, traced the wire's ends, and cut the remaining wire cord. The red camera light completely shut off immediately. I then proceeded to go upstairs, where I noticed another red camera light illuminating my bedroom, my bathroom, the guest bedrooms, and the hallway.

I could feel the whole house being bugged with cameras. I quickly began to hear Justin harass and taunt me outside of my house. I even looked out of the window to see a man aiming a gun directly at me through my window. Then I heard Justin, his sisters, and brothers stating that if I did not stop investigating what happened to my trust fund, they would kill me.

Later, I heard gunshots continuously. I had recently purchased a black powder .44 magnum gun, but I did not have access to this weapon. This led me to purchase another .44 magnum gun in order to protect my life and my home from these tyrants.

I decided to contact the police immediately. After telling the police exactly what had happened, they suggested that I relocate. So, I began to work on finding a new home for relocation. I kept a pistol close to me just in case Justin or his siblings decided to force themselves inside my house and come in illegally.

Justin and his family began bribing our neighbors with money and drugs to convince them that I was unstable, justifying their gang stalking, illegal surveillance, and harassment. My neighbors began to get involved with harassment and gang stalking, and this led to a deadly encounter and confrontation resulting from their participation in it.

One day, after being harassed, I decided I had enough of that and went over to talk to my neighbor and ask them why they were doing it. After walking over to their home, I began to be threatened by one of the neighbors. I asked the neighbor to talk to his son, who had been consistently harassing and aiding Justin.

The neighbor laughed, "What's my problem? They're not harassing me?" I told them I would protect myself and threatened to go to the police. Suddenly, a red sedan pulled up with six people threatening to attack me. Another car pulled up with five more people getting out and pulling their weapons out on me.

Darren Cubie

I did not bring my .44 Magnum, which was still in my home unloaded for just this purpose. I thought if I was going to be approached and gang stalked, it would be better if I did not pull my gun, which would result in a shootout between me and the neighbors.

So instead, I grabbed one of the wooden step boards and proceeded to strike the first three guys who walked up in the faces and heads. I was well-trained in self-defense and martial arts and knew the appropriate areas to strike: the face, the neck, the groin, the knee, and the throat.

So, I had no problem with using the board to protect myself. As they approached me and I begin to strike, they suddenly jumped back and decided to throw rocks instead of physically attacking with their fists. One rock broke my window, so I decided to pick up a brick and throw it as hard as I could to break through the back window of their car.

This led to the police being contacted. The police quickly came, and Justin and the neighbors decided to tell the police that they thought I was unstable due to the fact I attacked them. They stated they didn't know why I break through their car window.

That night, I decided to quickly move away from there. I decided not to go back to my home and instead go back to California to continue the investigation into my lost Bank of America trust funds in the amount of $875,000, which were located at 6300 Sunset Boulevard, Hollywood, California, 90028.

* * *

After arriving in Los Angeles, California, I made my way to Bank of America. This is where I had been shown my $875,000 trust fund during the IRS criminal investigations in 2005 by Bank of America manager Troy Gardner.

Troy showed me the computer printout, which indicated the balance, social security number, date of birth, and the name of the beneficiary of my account, which was me, Darren Cubie. So, I was sure that I would be able to locate the remaining balance of my trust fund account if I visited the same location at Bank of America. But to my surprise, they stated that Troy Gardner no longer worked there and had been moved to Santa Monica, California, on Flower Street. The bank manager told me that I would be better off going to Bank of America's Record archive division in San Francisco, California.

So, I decided to head to San Francisco, California; after arriving, I quickly went to the Bank of America's orchard division located there and then requested an account investigation search at the archive division of Bank of America.

I was not prepared for what was going to happen in this investigation, due to a limited number of financial resources, and I decided to use help from a community center located in San Francisco.

There was a lot more to encounter ahead, and I had to witness continued gang stalking by Justin Riviera and his family. This led to an encounter which was set up by Justin Riviera, his siblings, and aunt Margie Jones.

Jail Time

I also had a reasonable assumption based on what I heard from the remarks of Justin and his siblings when they mentioned Angie Yarbrough, my two sisters, and Marshall Thompson saying that they were going to kill me if I did not stop investigating into my hidden, lost trust fund.

I noticed subtle harassment until one day, while at the center, I was approached by an Asian man who decided to create a confrontation by calling me a nigger.

This was one of the same men who I'd seen Justin speaking to with his sisters and brothers.

I stood up and said, "What did you say to me?"

He said, "I said move nigger!" then he quickly punched me in my stomach. I responded by quickly punching him and knocking him over the table with one single hit to the eye.

Little did I know that this was going to become a matter of life and death and result in him attacking me with a knife, after stalking me the next day, in order to try to kill me.

While walking down three blocks from my house the same day, I turned around after feeling as if someone might be walking behind me. I noticed an Asian man dressed in jeans and a brown shirt, and a brown hat walking up close. I thought to myself, "This couldn't be the same person... he has completely different clothing on."

I said, "Are you the same guy that just left out of the community center and attacked me?"

This Asian man continued to walk closer and closer, then finally stating, "Look what you did to my eye, nigger."

I said, "It's over with. Let me just go about my business."

The Asian man replied, "I'm going to kill you, nigger."

I finally had enough of this and said, "Okay, let's finish this."

The Asian man quickly pulled a knife and launched directly at me several times, attempting to stab me to death. I quickly punched him in the face, grabbed his arm, which held the knife, pulled him to the ground, and struck him five times. Each strike, I said, "Put the knife down!"

After the last punch, I kicked him in his face and walked away.

I was unaware of the significant damage I inflicted upon him; after all, he attempted to stab me, and I had no other choice. I had attempted to walk away and avoid this confrontation completely, but he refused. So, I had no other choice but to defend myself.

Despite that, once I got past the first block ahead of me, I heard police sirens, turned around, and police officers told me to put my hands on top of my head as I was being placed under arrest.

I quickly responded, "Why am I being arrested? He attacked me with a knife; all I did was defend myself! I tried to walk away, but all I did was defend myself from being attacked by a man with a knife, who tried to stab me to death."

They said, "You're not under arrest. We're just taking you down for questioning." So, I went with them peacefully. I was to discover this wasn't anything but further from the truth, as a white female detective interrogated me about what happened and why. I quickly told her I was using the community center for resources while investigating what occurred to my lost trust fund account that my father from the music group Chi-Lites had left me.

During my attempts to use the facility at the community center, I got approached by an Asian man who verbally harassed me by calling me a nigger after punching me in my stomach because he wanted me to move my chair. I thought this would just be the end of the ordeal, but I was absolutely wrong to think that nothing would happen further. Under the circumstances of the trust fund theft, this was not going to be over until they could put me in prison and get me out of the way.

The detective came back and before I knew it, they had charged me with attempting premeditated murder with a deadly weapon, despite the fact I didn't have a weapon at all and the only weapon that was ever involved was the knife that this guy pulled on me.

I had no intention to murder anyone, let alone attempt to permanently injure. After all, I only struck him five times. I was told by the detective that this guy was in the emergency room and had to undergo surgery for over 13 fractures and metal plates to the face, including a broken jaw and broken eye sockets. I was shocked; I had even injured my own hand during this fight by striking the ground.

I was put in the jail infirmary awaiting trial. This was just a living nightmare. My worst fears confirmed that Justin and the others were setting me up for attempted murder. I was furious, but I knew that this was a setup!

So, I was mentally prepared for what lay ahead. To my surprise, my worst fears were confirmed after finding out that the COs had attempted to bribe both him and another person to start a confrontation and attack me in order to create a scenario that would allow the police to pull me out of the unit pod and into a psych pod. I was told this by two of the other inmates located in the same room during my time at the San Francisco jail.

While there I was harassed daily by an Asian man and other officers. I believe they were trying to set me up for a life sentence and get me to fight this man in order to convince the judge that I was violent and that it would be justifiable to keep me there and find me guilty on all counts. This case lasted over 15 months in total, and two trials were assigned to the leading public defender director, Matthew, and his assistant Elizabeth Hilton. Two trials and 15 months later, I was exonerated of justifiable self-defense and released.

Run-In With Justin: Part 2

I had been paying on a new house located in 9 Mile, Detroit, Michigan. This house was over 3,000 square feet and three stories. Although it was a fixer-upper, the home had great potential, and I was excited to be able to get to my new home in Detroit. Once I got to Detroit, I was shocked and dismayed that my home had been sold after I had put 50% down for the asking price of the house. I called the real estate company and agent and asked what happened to my house. She told me they had sold the house, and I would have to choose from three other homes that they had available. Furthermore, they said my money would be applied to whichever house I chose.

After I selected a home that I thought would be a good second choice, the real estate agent quickly persuaded me out of the house and convinced me to get a home located at 93 Edge Valve, Detroit, Michigan. I had no knowledge whatsoever about Michigan's neighborhoods or areas, and I didn't know whether it was a good neighborhood or not. Nevertheless, she continued to persuade me to obtain this home. After I told her I wanted the other house, she said "Oh, that house was very unsafe and we don't have the title deed to it. We would have problems getting the deed, so it's better to get the 93 Edge Valve home."

I decided to go ahead and take the offer once I returned back to Detroit, Michigan. As I got there, I noticed the home was on a secluded crime-infested street. I saw a woman standing on the corner who appeared to be a prostitute. I asked her if she knew where 93 Edge Valve Street was.

She stated, "Why do you want to know?"

I explained that I just bought the house. Then someone that looked like a drug dealer or pimp began walking up towards us. She quickly said, "Oh, he's just looking for a 93 Edge Valve."

The man asked why, so I said the same thing to him as I did the other woman. He replied, "Oh well, then it's right down the street." I knew right then that the street was trouble.

After walking inside the home and checking it out, I walked upstairs where I began to notice an odor. There was a strange smell as if a dead body had been inside the home for a long time. I could feel that someone had either died upstairs in one of the rooms or was killed and left inside.

I began to clean up the home. Shortly after that, the next-door neighbor walked up on my door and talked to me, stating that he knew the owner of the home who had died upstairs. He further said that he was the man who found him dead and called the police.

He insisted that he was a good man and was even a participant in the Million Man March on Washington. So, I said, "Oh, well nice to meet you," after a brief introduction of myself to him.

I can't explain how I felt some strange eerie feeling that this man was a liar and potentially even a drug dealer or murderer. Later, after about a month or two, I noticed that Justin and his sisters and brothers followed me to this home.

I saw them talking to the neighbor who had come over to my home and introduced himself. To my surprise, Justin moved into the very home the neighbor had rented out. I was able to hear Justin and his siblings harass and taunt me daily.

This home had been occupied and rented to a Caucasian woman with her sister and her boyfriend. Justin began to rent a room out of the home along with the sisters and brothers. I wasn't prepared for what I was about to see or endure, never knowing that this would lead to murder. The first murder began with the Caucasian white lady who was dating Justin and rented one of the rooms.

Eventually, the harassment got to such a degree that Justin began to place toxic gas chemicals into my pipeline outside. On one occasion, he had put so much toxic chemicals through my pipeline that I nearly passed out. My neighbor came running out of her home, screaming, "Get out of the house, get out of the house, he put poison gas in the pipes!"

Then on another occasion, he flooded my basement all the way up to the stairs. It took over two months to clear back into the drains. Not to mention he would shoot guns daily and threaten my life continuously from night to morning. He even used neighbors and drug dealers in the local 6 Mile area to sit on my porch and steps to intimidate me.

I remember walking out there, telling them to get off my porch, then firing several shots to let them know to stay off my property. Furthermore, if I continue to be harassed, I would defend myself and have the means to be able to do it.

The point was quickly understood by the drug dealers and gang stalkers who Justin and his family hired to harass and stalk me. But this didn't stop the consistent harassment daily.

* * *

On this last occasion which led to the death of this young lady, she begin to get into an argument which led to her threatening Justin by saying she did not want anything else to do with the gang stalking and harassment that he and the others have been doing towards me.

She told Justin, if he did not let her be alone and leave her out of it, she would go to the police and tell them everything that she knew about, including the trust fund theft that he and his family were attempting to steal while gang-stalking me.

This is what led to her death and murder. I heard Justin reply, "You're not going to the police and telling him anything."

Later Justin replied, "Darren, I had to kill her because of you," and "You made me kill her" as he began to cry.

The woman died, and later Justin's sister told him that he didn't need to do that.

His brother was also angry at him, telling him, "This was the last straw." Right after committing the murder, Justin started shouting, "Darren! Look what you made me do! You made me kill her, Darren!" Basically, he was blaming me for no reason. I wound up going to the police's office to report the activity because I knew what type of people they were.

Several days later, the DEA conducted a raid at Justin's house to arrest all the murder suspects, including Justin, upon finding out that the house was basically a trap house. Essentially, what he really wanted to do was fund the drug dealer's activity in the city and nearby areas. Justin was probably looking forward to starting some criminal business of his own by using my money as finance for the activity.

Just before the raid took place, Justin escaped. He had hacked my phone and had access to all my information and calls, knowing quite well about the DEA's raid and arrest much before it had happened. The day before the raid, the gang was threatening to kill me if I hadn't given them the money from the trust fund.

Justin had shifted to the house right next to the one being raided. During the raid, he came outside my house and knocked on the door. After finding my gun, I started shooting at the door which made the DEA believe that I was shooting at them. An entire SWAT team was called and approximately 30 police team members showed up to arrest me. I told them everything and clarified what just happened along with the threats that were taking place.

* * *

A week or two passed and I was coming from my college in a cab, when the cab driver said to me, "Oh, that's the street where they found the dead white girl that was left located in an alley. The police said she died from an axe to her head." I immediately got reminded of the white lady that Justin had been dating. This was the girlfriend that he killed after she told him she would go to the police if he did not let her out of any involvement in harassment.

I attempted to file a police report both online and on the phone. Later, I noticed another murder done by Justin and the criminals located at that house. I was coming back from a local service station and decided to take a shortcut across the street to my house while walking through an alley. I noticed one of the same guys, who Justin hung around with, lying dead in the alley.

At first, it looked like a body of a man that stood about 6'3, laying in the alley with a black sleeping bag over his body. As I walked closer, I saw a dead man with a black body bag wrapped around his body. As I walked closer, I noticed a black lady holding a purse, stating that he was just drunk. Later, she said, "Oh, you must think he's dead too."

I replied, "Oh no, I just thought he was sleep and I was about to give him some money." I did notice a funeral home Hirsch car waiting at the service station next to the alley, but I did not pay much attention to it or what it was doing there.

This lady began to look very suspicious towards me and reached inside of her purse. She began to go deeper and deeper into her purse as if she was going to grab a gun to shoot me.

"Oh okay, well if he's just drunk, I'll just go my way," I said quickly then left.

Once I got home, I realized that the man who was murdered had been the same man who would argue with Justin about harassing me over the trust fund. I even attempted to contact the police and let them know what was happening.

So, the police said that they would come by and take a look at it. I called back about an hour later to hear that they found nothing. They sent a squad car to check out where the dead man's body was located. I quickly realized that it was time to move from that location. Justin had not only gang-stalked me but had murdered several people as well.

Even during my attempts to finish my college education while living in Flint, Michigan, my college records had been hacked by Justin and his family and friends. That's when I moved to Flint, Michigan, where I now reside.

Acknowledgments

Thank you to God Almighty for without Him, I would not have the strength, mind, courage, morals, values, or integrity to continue my fight. Thank you, God Almighty!

I would first like to acknowledge the tremendous amount of talent of my father, Creadel Jones. His tremendous effort in becoming one of the greatest musical talents in R&B music history is commendable, and I could not be prouder. My father's dedication to perfecting his career and his talent in the music industry has been inspirational.

I also would like to acknowledge my mother, Deborah Jones, and her loving inspiration, understanding, faithfulness, determination in helping support my father throughout his entertainment career. I also want to acknowledge her loyalty to her husband, my beloved father Mr. Creadel Jones, our entire Chi-Lites family, and each of her children, which included my two sisters and me. She played a significant role in our family.

May both of them rest in peace.

My last acknowledgment is to Bishop Cornell Hennings and his beautiful wife, Mrs. Ernestine Hennings, and their relentless concern, love, and support. Thank you.

About the Author: Darren Cubie

Parents:

Creadel Jones and Deborah Jones

Birthplace:

St. Louis, Missouri

Education:

University of National Louis University Born:

Founder:

Entertainers Against Exploitation

Appearances:

Judge Lauren Lake Paternity Court Television, 2014

Rick Wade Show, 2000

Darren Cubie, the son of an R&B legend, tells the incredible true story of a family torn apart by greed, corruption, and the systematic abuse of Black artists in the United States. Darren grew up in St. Louis not knowing why assassination attempts, FBI investigations, and witness protection programs weren't supposed to be a normal part of life.

The hall-of-fame success of the iconic soul group known as the Chi-Lites came at a terrible price for Darren's father, founding member Creadel "Red" Jones. Like so many other Black artists of the day, the devil was in the details in the form of contracts and agreements with the mob filtered through corrupt record executives and banksters. The bitter ending of Creadel's journey in 1994, penniless on the streets of L.A., spurred Darren to become a champion for artists everywhere who've suffered from this decades-old system of abuse.

Darren Cubie

www.ingramcontent.com/pod-product-compliance
Lightning Source LLC
Chambersburg PA
CBHW030225170426
43194CB00007BA/865